Repentance
A thought for each day of the year

Philip M. Hudson

Copyright 2019 by Philip M. Hudson.

Published 2019.

Printed in the United States of America.

All rights reserved.

No portion of this book may be reproduced, stored in a retrieval system, or transmitted in any form or by any means - electronic, mechanical, photocopy, recording, scanning, or other - except for brief quotations in critical reviews or articles, without the prior written permission of the author.

ISBN 978-1-950647-20-0

Illustrations - Google Images.

This book may be ordered from online bookstores.

Publishing Services by BookCrafters
Parker, Colorado.
www.bookcrafters.net

Table of Contents

Acknowledgements..i
Preface..v
Introduction..vii

A Thought For Each Day Of The Year..1
About The Author...367
By The Author...369
What More Can I Say?..373

Nephi clearly taught that "it is by grace that we are saved, after all we can do." (2 Nephi 25:23). Latter-day Saints, however, sometimes emphasize works to the point that it may seem to others that the grace of God takes a back seat to their own efforts to earn salvation.

Acknowledgements

In this volume, I have attributed quotations to original authors whenever possible, as well as when I have editorialized their ideas. In many cases, however, my language will naturally reflect the teachings of leaders and members of The Church of Jesus Christ of Latter-day Saints.

The list of those who have contributed to this book is endless. As I have organized my own thoughts, I have realized how heavily I have borrowed from the towering examples of those who, over the years, have been my mystical mentors, my sensible chaperones, my spiritual guides, my surrogate saviors, my compassionate critics, and everything in between.

They are my avatars, manifestations of deity in bodily forms, my na'vi, the visionaries, who communicate with God on a level to which I can only aspire, and my tsaddik, whom I esteem as intuitive interpreters of biblical law and scripture. They are my divine teachers incarnate. They have offered listening ears, extended open arms, lifted my spirits, shown me the way, stretched my mind, reinforced my faith, strengthened my testimony, helped me to discover my wings, given immaterial support, provided of their means, emboldened me with words of encouragement, cheered me on with wise counsel, taught me humility, been there to steady me, soothed my troubled soul, stepped in to nurture me, led me to fountains of living water, wet my parched lips with inspired counsel, and bound up my wounds.

When I think of the influence of a multitude of angels thinly disguised as my family, friends, and peers, I remember the words of Sir Isaac Newton, who, when pressed to reveal the great secret behind his accomplishments, simply replied: "I stood on the shoulders of giants." Of course, at the end of the day, I alone am responsible for the content of this volume. But I hope my interpretations of principles and doctrine will cultivate your interest to dig deeper into the themes woven into this tapestry, by turning to the scriptures and seeking inspiration from the Spirit. My only goal is to help you to expand your insights into the telestial mile markers, the terrestrial truths, and the celestial guidelines that accompany each of us during our quest for enlightenment through the miracle of the Atonement.

The elements
of God's Plan speak
to our spirits, for every
Gospel principle carries within
itself a witness that it is true. Its
language is universal, and when our
minds have been illuminated by faith,
we enjoy fluency, familiarity, and an
easy comfort with the revealed word
of God that opens up vistas of
eternal proportion before
our eyes.

It is faith that captures the heart of a little child before it has been exposed to the cankering influence and corrosive elements of the world, before their hearts are set upon temporal things, and their spirituality has been so weakened that the things of God are no longer part of their daily experience. Better than the rest of us, little children have a capacity to "lay aside the things of this world, and seek for the things of a better." (D&C 25:10).

Preface

I love to learn by reading the scriptures, and I often think of St. Hilary, who wrote in the third century: "Scripture consists not in what we read, but in what we understand." In each of the musings within this volume, I have consistently tried to find a scriptural foundation and a spiritual confirmation as I put my pen to paper.

I am continually reminded of Nephi's counsel to press forward with complete dedication and steadfastness, or confidence with a firm determination in Christ, having a perfect brightness of hope, or perfect faith, and charity, or a love of God and of all men. If we do this, feasting upon the word of Christ, or receiving strength and nourishment as we ponder the doctrines of the kingdom, and particularly the principle of repentance, and as we then endure to the end in righteousness, we shall have eternal life, which is the greatest of God's gifts. (See 2 Nephi 31:20).

It is with love, then, that I extend to you the invitation to enjoy this omnibus of random thoughts. Embrace it at face value, and use its exhortations to repentance as a springboard to your own personal plateaus of discovery, as you are taught by the Spirit to move in the direction of your dreams.

Repentance follows
an established pattern.
"Ask for the old paths, where
is the good way, and walk therein,
and ye shall find rest for your
souls." (Jeremiah 6:16).

Introduction

If they are fortunate, novice quilters quickly learn a bit of wisdom from the Amish, who make some of the finest quilts in the world. On purpose, the Amish build mistakes into their projects, because they believe that any attempt on their part to design and produce a flawless creation would be a mockery of God, Who alone is perfect. The humility of the Amish makes me think of my own weak attempts to put the thoughts expressed in this omnibus to paper. In His infinite wisdom, God knows very well that I do not need to consciously plan on lacing my efforts with errors. That will come quite naturally, without the need for me to intentionally contribute to my short-comings.

Perhaps this serendipitous collection of musings will do little more than help to define quirks in my personality. Each of us is different, and many things, including our family and friends, the circumstances in which we find ourselves, the quality of our education, and our own personalities, inspire and mold our oral and written expressions. I would like to think that, in this text, all of these influences have been encouraging, affirmative, and constructive.

The reflections within this tome leave the door ajar for the reader, to allow shafts of the light of understanding to creep in. If, as I have expressed my thoughts, I mis-stated myself a few times, or flat-out got it wrong, I ask the patient indulgence and gentle correction of the reader.

Too often, I realize that my communications can be "carefully disguised with hypocrisy and glittering words," as Einstein put it. Although I do fancy myself a wordsmith, I have tried to avoid pedestrian expressions, idle language, and lazy scholarship. I do not pretend to be an authority on the principle of repentance, inasmuch as I believe that we are all works in progress, but if you find the factual tone of a particular musing disengaging, the truth is that I typically experienced a deep personal involvement in my interpretation of the principles that illuminated its meaning.

In any event, when you open this volume, I hope you ponder these minute musings with as much enjoyment as I have experienced while creating them.

Pride is motivated by self-will, while repentance is inspired by God's will. Pride is driven by the fear of man, while repentance is nurtured by the love of God. The applause of the world rings loudly in the ears of the prideful, but it is the accolades of heaven that warm the hearts of the repentant faithful.

In truth,
those who refuse
to repent have more
won't power than
will power.

As we quietly repent, the righteousness of our efforts will be revealed in spectacular simplicity and plainness. The walls of opposition to our purposeful repentance will crumble and fall away. In our efforts, the Lord will comfort and succor us with the bread of life. As we journey through the harsh and unforgiving environment of mortality, seeking the Lord while He may be found, oases will spring up in the desert and living water will slake our thirst.

Unlike the repentant, those who are proud are more comfortable with their own perception of truth than they are with God's omniscience. They pit their own abilities against His priesthood power, their own paltry overtures against His mighty works, and their stubborn will against His gentle counsel.

Unlike the repentant, the proud stubbornly hold to their own opinions rather than yielding themselves to God's direction. They fill their own lamps with oil, but are penurious when sharing their wealth with others.

As we repent, we nurture our relationship with God and the Holy Ghost. We become the fashioners of our fortunes, even as we learn to rely upon reserves that are only found in Jesus Christ, and that we quite pleasantly find are greater than ourselves.

Those who
are enamored with
themselves will never
experience the mind
and soul expanding
epiphany that they
are less than the
dust of the
earth.

Not only can
our travel plans
be spoiled, but also
the direction of our
life's journey itself can
be detoured if we yield
to the temptation offered
by telestial treats that
seem just too good
to be true.

The first step in the process of our repentance is a tipping point at which we consciously recognize our sins. The second step is our clear understanding of Justice, Mercy, and the grace of God, and our appreciation of the relationship between them because of The Plan of Deliverance From Death.

Our
redemption
requires that we
enjoy a familiarity
with the Way, the Truth,
and the Life, or, in other
words, that we have direct
experience with God, with
Jesus Christ and with
the Holy Ghost.

Satan, who was a liar from
the beginning, even now continues
his efforts to foil The Plan of Salvation
by the substitution of his own counterfeit,
unworkable alternative that would not
require repentance or the Atonement.
Fortunately, in the setting of the
Council in Heaven, we were
able to see through his
deception. We still
do.

When we
turn our backs
on the invitation to
have a relationship with
God and remain alienated
from Him by spiritual death, it
is unavoidable that we must
eventually surrender to
inclinations that are
carnal, sensual,
and devilish.

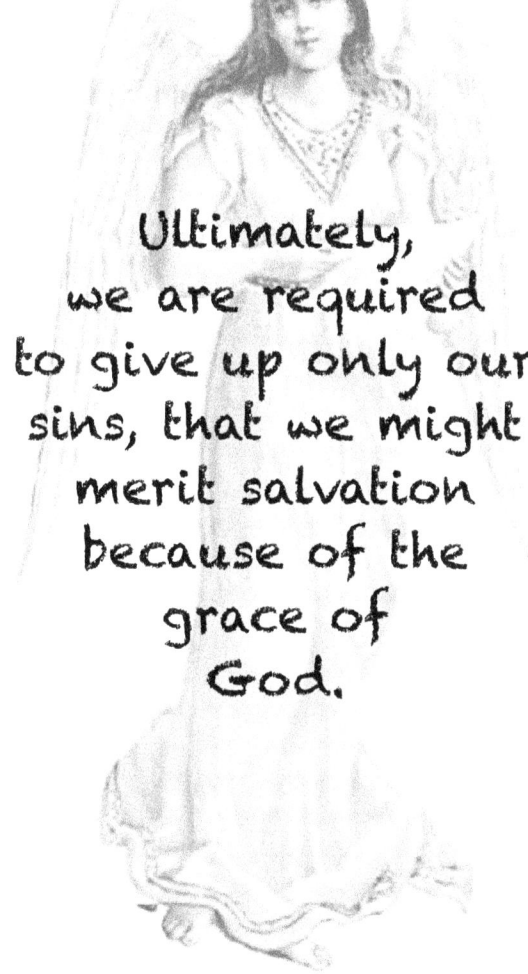

Ultimately, we are required to give up only our sins, that we might merit salvation because of the grace of God.

Those
who repent are
long-suffering and
they are faithful. When
things seem that they could
be no worse, they are at their
best, because then they are
particularly sensitive to
the comfort that comes
thru the whisperings
of the Spirit.

Without
repentance,
we are free to
negotiate our way
thru the minefields
of mortality. However,
as we do, forsaking help
where it may be found,
we will look like an
octopus on roller
skates.

When we have been
quickened by the Spirit,
we recognize the source of
the life-giving water that is
offered, and we accept in our
hearts the sacrifice of the Savior,
manifest in His Atonement. When we
transgress, we speedily repent and
return unto God, to find favor in
His sight; to have our blessings,
that He is anxious to restore,
poured out once again
upon our heads.

We don't try to fix everything all at once. The next life is required to achieve perfection. For the time being, we content ourselves to learn by "precept upon precept; line upon line; here a little, and there a little." (Isaiah 28:10). Doing so, we are given "consolation by holding forth that which is to come, confirming our hope!" (D&C 128:21).

The
blueprints
of Babylon are
always drawn with
a stylus that is moved
by the unsteady hands of
Beelzebub's architects
of anarchy and
creators of
chaos.

It is when
we have known
hardship that we
develop empathy, are
more likely to overlook
the shortcomings of others,
and are quicker to forgive them
their trespasses. By learning to
avoid being judgmental, and
by developing benevolent
blindness, we are better
able to help others to
meet their own
challenges.

Unlike
the repentant,
those who are prideful
seek after signs. Because
they are past feeling, they
require greater and greater
intensities of stimulation to
receive the same level of
temporal or theological
gratification. What they
have been given is
never enough.

"These
six things
doth the Lord
hate: yea, seven are
an abomination unto him: A
proud look, a lying tongue, and
hands that shed innocent blood, an
heart that deviseth wicked imaginations,
feet that be swift in running to mischief, a
false witness that speaketh lies, and he
that soweth discord among brethren."
(Proverbs 6:16-19).

Those
of weak
will, who are
swift in running
to mischief, forfeit
their desire to repent,
although they may not even
be aware of it. They lose their
focus, just as eyesight may be lost
over time. First they squint, and then
they hold the page a little closer or a
little further away, compensating for the
inability to see clearly. It doesn't matter
whether it is the printed page or their
integrity that they cannot read. In
each case, there is a character
crippling compromise.

We know by the
casualty count from the
ideological War in Heaven, that
some of Heavenly Father's children
forfeit their privilege to obtain a body.
For those who remained faithful in the
pre-earth existence, however, came
humbling liabilities, and so The
Plan required the Creator to
die for our sins, only
conditional upon
repentance.

Repentance is like a stethoscope that gauges the vital capacity of our prideful hearts. They must be broken in contrition in order to exhibit the steady sinus rhythm that confirms perfect harmony with proven principles of perfection.

Even when we
are fully committed,
repentance can bless us
with repetitive moments of
confirmation, when we can say,
as did members of the Church in
Zarahemla, that through the miracle
of forgiveness, by the power of the
Atonement, our hearts have once
again been changed through
faith on His name.

With repentance,
our spiritual bank
accounts overflow with
deposits that may later be
withdrawn as an annuity
of joy in the kingdom
of heaven.

We
rely upon the
benevolent blindness
of God when we plead for
forgiveness of our trespasses.
He asks us to be benevolently
blind when we are tempted
to judge others with
harshness.

It is challenging to muster faith unto repentance that leads us to the strait and narrow gate of baptism. In fact, "few there be that find it." (Matthew 7:14).

It is only in unrepentant Babylon that the Devil is able to exult in his role as the de-facto god of this earth.

Because of
repentance, when
we find our way back
to our heavenly home, we
may still be clothed in our
tangible trappings, but we will
also be arrayed with the power
and authority of metaphysical
vestments that nurture the
intrinsic light that had
always flickered
from within
us.

To really
take advantage of
their temporal travels and
to put a positive spin on their
telestial trials, Latter-day Saints
have learned to repent, that they
might in a coming day be restored
to their proper and perfect frame,
ultimately to face their destiny,
clothed in glory, immortality,
and eternal life.

Repentance
draws upon positive
energy and channels
it into a force that
expands the sphere
of influence of
the Savior.

Sometimes,
the power of
the Atonement
needs to be felt
through suffering.
As Paul wrote: "For
unto you it is given
in behalf of Christ,
not only to believe
on him, but also
to suffer for
his sake."

As the
world descends into
anarchy, and allows itself
to becomes distracted by the
idol worship of invention as
well as by the pagan gods
of its own construction,
it is ripe to also be
led into spiritual
bondage.

"Once, there was a little girl who had a little curl right in the middle of her forehead. When she was good, she was very good. And when she was bad, guess what? Her Father loved her all the same."

Repentance can catalyze our relationship with God, when it unshackles us from the icy grip of our captivity to Satan; and all is because of the Atonement of Christ.

When
we are born
again through
repentance, our
orientation is more
toward the expansive
laws of the eternal world
than it is to the restrictive
confines of our physical
surroundings. This is
why our spirits are
nurtured through
repentance.

When our weakness is linked to repentance, it can actually be motivating, as we positively respond to the invitation to do better, and to be kinder; to be more merciful and more forgiving.

The
raw and ugly
contamination of sin
is incompatible with the
uncompromising standard of
spiritual hygiene that is required
of those who, one day, hope to
inhabit heaven and live in
the company of God
and angels.

We are
assaulted
daily by the
Seven Deadly
Sins, and to some
degree, we all find
ourselves susceptible to
their influences. In every
case, however, the Atonement
of Christ stands ready to rescue
us. Repentance rekindles our zest
for life by reviving our enthusiasm,
restoring our divine inspiration, and
recalibrating the celestial compass
that rests within each of our
beating hearts.

As we
determine to
repent, we can learn
to be humble by receiving
chastisement and counsel, by
forgiving those who have offended
us, by rendering service, and by our
good example that teaches others
to do as our Heavenly Father
would have them do.

When our
character has
been tainted by
pride, its salvation
lies in repentance. When
we look around us to argue
who is right, repentance
stands ready to look
up to God to ask
what is right.

Repentance fosters an atmosphere of collaboration, conciliation, and cooperation, and encourages us to share our resources with others in order to achieve solutions to our problems that are to our mutual advantage.

Conformity to
God's laws has the
capacity to generate
confidence, as we feel
ourselves being lifted
upward as upon the
wings of eagles.

No matter
how ponderous
the burden is that we
have created due to our
inattention to our spiritual
well-being, Jesus Christ, Who
is the mediator of a heavenly
Weight-Watcher Program,
will lift us up at the
last day.

When our hearts
are hardened against
the invitation to repent,
it is as though our portion
has been diminished further
and further, until our natural
defenses against the aggressive
tactics of the Devil crumble,
and we are left to fight
our battles all by
ourselves.

Those who decline
the offer of the riches
of eternity that have been
unfolded to their view by
the power of the Atonement
are doomed to live their
lives in scarcity of their
basic spiritual needs.

Repentance
enables us to
successfully flex
our spiritual muscles
and exercise our moral
agency in a forum of free
will that confidently engages
opposition in a vigorous
tug-of-war.

The unrepentant wicked can only conduct their lives in opposition to the laws of heaven for so long, before critical mass is reached. At that point, a readjustment is required to bring the disobedient back into harmonious balance with nature.

It is our
repentance that can
neutralize the negative
aspects of the opposition
that has been designed as
a key to the success of the
Plan. It harmonizes the trials
we all face in our every-day
experiences with the blessings
that have been reserved for
the repentant faithful who
will inhabit the mansions
above, that have been
prepared for them
by our Father
in Heaven.

Ultimately,
the power of
Mercy to redeem
us is generated in
the fiery-hot crucible
of adversity, for we
receive no witness
until after the
trial of our
faith.

Isaiah may
have been alluding
to the repentant, when he
exhorted Israel: "Say to the
prisoners, go forth (and) to
them that are in darkness,
shew yourselves ... Their
pastures shall be in
all high places."
(Isaiah 49:9).

As we follow
the path that leads
to happiness, we make
frequent stops at sites that
are prominently marked by
signs that invite us to pause for
repentance, refreshment, and
recommitment to proven
principles.

The vision of
our potential is
unclouded by the
myopia of manner,
the cloudy cataracts
of convention, or the
presbyopia of procedure.
When we are at our very
best, we can begin to
appreciate the all-
seeing eye of
Jehovah.

As we listen
to the prophets who
cry repentance, we feel
that "whoever speaks to us
in the right voice, him or her
we shall follow as the waters
follow the moon. We do so
silently, and with fluid
steps anywhere around
the globe." (Walt
Whitman).

If
we look
closely, woven
within the fabric
of the material that
makes up the tapestry
of repentance, there are
sometimes "dark threads
that are as needful in the
Weaver's skillful hand as
the threads of gold and
silver, in the pattern
He has planned."
(B. Franklin).

When life throws us a curve, and we go south when the path goes north, we need to remember to "Just get back on the bike."

The Day
of Judgment
does not lie over
a distant horizon, but is
today. We speak, think, and
act according to the celestial,
terrestrial, or telestial laws that
are before us. Just as a barometer
is used to measure the direction
in which the weather is headed,
our capacity for repentance
helps us to be continually
aware of the direction we
must follow if we hope
to regain the shelter
of our heavenly
home.

Sometimes,
it is only when
we have enrolled
in the graduate school
of hard knocks, and have
pre-paid the required tuition,
that we obtain the credits that
are earned by obedience to the
curriculum, learn how to show
charity to our brothers and
sisters, and forgive others
as the Savior forgives
us our trespasses.

Our acceptance of the absolute necessity of the principle of opposition within the operating guidelines of The Plan does not give us license to act recklessly or to capitulate to the Dark Side, and to somehow avoid immediate accountability.

The only payment required for the gift of salvation is the heart and a willing mind. The only things that we must give up are our sins.

Timid souls who are cautiously hesitant and tentatively faithful don't consciously intend to lose the desire to repent. Testimony just fades away, like a slow leak in an automobile tire, and not as a blowout. But, it may often be traced back to the tendency to mischief that may have taken root during a time period of particularly intense vulnerability to the wiles of the Devil.

It is to our benefit that
we become acquainted with
evil as well as with good, with
pain as well as with pleasure, and
with darkness as well as with light;
with error as well as with truth, and
with punishment for the infraction of
God's eternal laws, as well as with the
blessings that follow our obedience.
Mortality was designed to be our
only opportunity to have these
character-building life
experiences.

The
invitation
to forgive and
to be forgiven is
juxtaposed against
the sense of despair,
despondency, distress,
and the deprivation that
go hand-in-hand with our
mortal schooling. These
are brutal examples of
the opposition in all
things that is part
of the package
that we call
life.

It makes
little difference
to our Father in Heaven
whether we are combating the
influences of the Seven Deadly
Sins, or the garden-variety of
transgressions that we commit
every day; the doctrine of the
Atonement stipulates that we
go through the process of
repentance when we fall
short of obedience to
all of the laws
of God.

Forgiveness
of sins through
repentance is based
upon our understanding
of the Atonement, which is
why it surely formed the basis
of our pre-mortal classroom
curriculum. The initiative is
now ours, to experience
religious recognition,
or the re-knowing
of what we have
beforehand
learned.

We may be surprised to find that our enduring to the end simply involves mastery of two principles: repentance for our own sins, and forgiveness of others.

As
soon as
we repent, we
are replenished by
the high octane fuel
of our faith. It ignites
the fire of our fortitude as
it propels us upward toward
our date with destiny where
heaven is waiting for us
to claim our eternal
reward.

It is our repentance that generates repetitive opportunities to smell the delicious aroma of the bread of life that is baking in a heavenly oven, as we steadily move along on the path that leads to the threshold of our celestial home.

Because we don't notice our poor spiritual fitness, we fail to repent. Our neglect fogs the mirror on our soul when we step out of the shower.

Without purposeful repentance, we cannot reasonably expect to inherit the glory of celestial realms; especially if we have aforetime been agreeable to abide by only telestial or terrestrial principles that put fewer demands upon our discipleship.

Truly did Shakespeare muse: "All the world's a stage," for life is a Three Act Play, and with our repentance, we become willing participants in a drama whose script was set in stone even before the earth upon which we live fell into existence.

When we
refuse to take
advantage of the
opportunity to repent,
we become deadened to
the better angels of our
nature and we lose our
capacity to touch and
feel the power of
the Atonement
with our
spirit.

As we put on the whole armour of God, the infinite and eternal Atonement of Jesus Christ is the only weapon we will need in our arsenal, in order to vanquish Satan. In our hearts, our knowledge of Gospel doctrine re-enthrones the Savior as the God of this earth.

Agency and opposition are powerful forces that constantly refine us by pushing, pulling, and tearing away at us within the crucible of experience. On our own, we cannot eliminate the consequences of sin. For that to happen, our Heavenly Father provided us with the Redeemer of Israel, even the Lamb slain from the foundation of the world.

Thank God
for the principle of
repentance that helps us
to get thru each day, and
comforts us during every
long night of darkness,
throughout our lives.
Truly, God stays up
late, and leaves a
light burning for
us, to guide us
Home.

In our obedience,
we try to be perfect in
our repentance, that God
might give unto us the spirit
of wisdom and of revelation,
to enlighten our understanding,
that we might embrace the hope
of the high calling of Jesus
Christ, and that the riches
of glory might abide as
our inheritance.

Every time we call upon God, we are, in effect, touching His garment. Just how our salvation is accomplished no-one can describe, for it can only be experienced by those who have known the exhilaration of receiving forgiveness of sin.

Repentance
is a tuning fork
that resonates on a
fundamental level with
elemental patterns that
are in harmony with truth.
We use it as we create
perfect pitch in our
quest to become
holy.

A spiritual
transformation
that follows our
heartfelt repentance
insures that we will enjoy
the fruits of a metaphorical
manipulation with an element
of rhetorical analogy: "Though
(our) sins be as scarlet, they shall
be as white as snow; though they
be red like crimson, they shall
be as wool." (Isaiah 1:18).

When we
are dealing
with weaknesses
in our contractions
that push forward the
Lord's agenda, relying on
the power of the Atonement
and considering the efficacy
of repentance quickens us to
bear our solemn witness with
renewed conviction, to the
convincing of both the
Jew and Gentile.

Repentance
binds us to heaven by
creating a pulsing stream
of inspiration whose flow has
no temporal boundary and
no spatial limitation. We
are at one with the
mind and will
of God.

If we repent, we never thirst, because we are anchored through Gospel topsoil into His fountain of living water. Repentance is the expression of our honesty with ourselves, with our Heavenly Father, and with the Savior, and with the Holy Ghost.

Eternal
life is gained by
redemption, and not
by the overpowering of
angels of Justice who
wield flaming
swords.

When we repent, we are inspired to enjoy feelings of serenity and harmony, in ways that were thoughtfully programmed by our Heavenly Father to touch our heart strings.

Wresting
the scriptures,
and suggesting that
we are saved by works,
twists holy writ from its
true or proper signification,
and perverts it from its
correct application.
Make no mistake
about it; we
all need to
repent.

Our
progress now
and in eternity
hinges largely upon
what we do with the
Atonement, and
upon what the
Atonement
does for
us.

As we exercise the
principle of repentance,
we reestablish synchronicity
with God's divine design. It
is His majestic clockwork
that has been calibrated
to coordinate with the
temporal pattern
of heaven
itself.

God's
exhortation
to repent asks us
to take a step or two
into the dark, that our
faith, which is our spiritual
strong searchlight, might be
activated to illuminate every
pothole, and every stone
that lies strewn along
the path that lies
before us.

Hope is
the unalterable
reward of our well-
founded faith, and is
the interest we accrue on
the investment made in our
undeviating trust in God, in
the principle of repentance,
and in His self-confident
promise of His power
to save us from
our follies.

When we have
allowed ourselves to
become soiled by the stain of
sin, spiritual death alienates us
from God. Mortality, however, is a
blessing, for it was envisioned as a
preparatory state, to permit us to
embrace the behavioral lifestyle
and quality of repentance that
is required for redemption, so
that we may return to the
presence of God, holy
and without spot.

God
glories in
the possibility
that we may become
like Him, which may be
the ultimate expression of
His matchless grace. "If ye by
the grace of God are perfect in
Christ, ... then are ye sanctified in
Christ by the grace of God ... unto
the remission of your sins, that
ye become holy, without spot."
(Moroni 10:33).

Forgiveness takes us on a journey that leads us into the uncharted and possibly unfamiliar territory of charity, the supernal characteristic of those who would call themselves disciples of Christ.

In the process
of our repentance,
we follow a natural
progression, but the real
power that stems from the
Atonement and saves us from
our sins hinges upon a deeper
and more abiding faith. It
is "the substance of things
hoped for, the evidence
of things not seen."
(Hebrews 11:1).

It is true that some of the blessings that are associated with repentance are literally out of this world and are reserved for those who will enjoy eternal life in the heavens above.

Those stubborn souls who doggedly refuse to repent by confessing their sins to Deity repeatedly look elsewhere for gods of wood and stone that may temporarily soothe their temporal trauma, but that can never permanently redeem them from their misery.

All of us
are repeatedly
faced with occasions
when withdrawals must be
made from our spiritual bank
accounts. When we rely upon the
Atonement, we put the principle of
repentance to its ultimate test. We do
not write checks that cannot be cashed.
We know that only after regular deposits
have been made over a period of time,
can we rely upon the cornucopia of
comfort created by the cushion of
confidence that is a currency
flowing from conduct that
is consistent with the
core curriculum of
contrition.

If we
ignore the
influences of
the Light of Christ
and the Holy Ghost that
nurture our innate urge to
abhor mischief, but instead allow
ourselves to be habitually distracted
by trifling concerns, we sin by omission
and risk settling for life in a marshland
of mediocrity that quickly degenerates
into the quicksand of sin, from
which there is no easy
escape.

Habitual
sin is a quicksand
that mires the unwary in
a monotonously repetitive and
underwhelming convention, and
in a mind-numbing conformity.
These are the opposites of the
imaginative spontaneity and
refreshingly distinctive
artistic individuality
of disciples of
Christ.

From a position of power, the Savior has negotiated with Justice to purchase our sins with the legally recognized currency of the Atonement. His voluntary act of sacrifice is perfectly balanced and attuned to accomplish the task at hand, to overcome death and hell, which are the opposites of eternal life and heavenly glory in the kingdom of our Father.

The principles of the Gospel intuitively draw us close to divine characteristics that cause us to shrink from sin and even to think of it as repulsive.

The Atonement can save us from our natural state of carnality, sensuality, and devilish inclinations. It activates the Law of Mercy, which mitigates for those who conform to its requirements the effects of the first Law, that demands Justice. It lifts us to a state of holiness, spirituality, angelic innocence, and happiness. It prepares us to feel comfortable in our heavenly home, where we will find ourselves in the presence of angels softly singing celestial lullabies that express only love.

Agency
and opposition
are always before
us, and repentance
stands as a sacred
sentinel, beckoning
us to enter in at
heaven's gate,
to find the
Rest of
God.

Those who
settle for the moral
mediocrity of character
crippling personality traits
can never get enough of what
they don't need, because
what they don't need
won't satisfy them.

Pride asks: "What do I want out of life?" while repentance meekly inquires: "What would God have me do?"

Perhaps it is only when he has hit rock-bottom, that the natural man hears an awful noise ringing in his ears as the whole earth groans under the weight of his iniquity.

Our
salvation
has less to do
with cherubim and a
flaming sword, and
more to do with
mercy and our
redemption.

If we could participate in the spiritual equivalent of Weight Watchers, we would have less trouble sleeping, less difficulty focusing, and less of a problem concentrating on the principle of repentance.

The arrogant,
boastful, conceited,
haughty, and self-centered
nature of the proud is easily
overpowered by the altruistic,
deferential, and self-effacing
behavior of the repentant,
whose firm grasp on the
horns of sanctuary
confirms their
faith in the
power of
God.

In our day, the electronic media gets in the way of our relationship with the Holy Ghost that has always been fundamental to the successful execution of the celestial principle of repentance.

Faith is
an essential
element of our
strategy of success,
because it lies at the
foundation of our hope
in Christ, with the assurance
of peace and the comfort of
our convictions that there is a
momentum in our lives that will
carry us, through our repentance,
on a trajectory that will streak
across the sky as it arches
heavenward.

The words repent and repentance are found in the Bible just 101 times. It seems that Heavenly Father has chosen to emphasize the importance of repentance in our day, since it is mentioned 450 times in the other standard works.

All are
equal in the
sight of God,
because of the
leveling influence
of repentance. The
Lord esteems all flesh
as one, but it is those
who are righteous
who find favor
in His sight.

With the
Restoration
of the Gospel,
the principle of
repentance became
a homing beacon. It
reignited the torch of
truth. Once again, as was
the custom in the apostolic
age, we listen to the quiet
stirrings of the Spirit, as
angels attend to our
most basic needs.

Everyone on earth is intuitively led to repentance. It is universally understood, is immune to conventional wisdom and cultural bias, and resists dogmatic interpretation. It also withstands the twisted influence of the private interpretation of the unenlightened.

We read in
the scriptures
how the Lord was
moved to observe of
the Saints in Zion that
they were rightly humble
and sought diligently to
learn wisdom and to find
truth. We are repeatedly
counseled to trust the
Lord and not to rely
upon our own
intellect.

Repentance is a brilliant beacon that has been provided at the end of the tunnel to guide those whose minds have been "blinded by the subtle craftiness of men." (D&C 123:12). Today, we have "a light that shineth in a dark place, until the day dawn, and the day star arise in (our) hearts." (2 Peter 1:19).

Because of our repentance, when we discard the trappings of mortality, "every limb and joint shall be restored to its body; yea, even a hair of the head shall not be lost; but all things shall be restored to their proper and perfect frame." (Alma 40:23).

Our Lord and
Savior taught that
His Gospel consists of
"repentance and baptism
by water, and then cometh
the baptism of fire and the
Holy Ghost … which showeth
all things, and teacheth
the peaceable things
of the kingdom."
(D&C 39:6).

When
repentance is
the fire fueling
our determination
to follow the Savior,
His Atonement charges
our spiritual batteries to
energize our vision with
infinite perspective.
We can be holy
and without
spot.

Repentance
is a principle that
can only be tested when
we nurture a companionship
with the Spirit, for when we
fall under its spell, we
are at-one with the
Savior of the
world.

When
Adam and
Eve transgressed
God's law in the Garden
of Eden, it was not because
they were weak, but because
they were strong. Our first
parents were spiritual
giants. They were
mighty oaks;
we are but
acorns.

Blind opposition, enmity, hatred, hostility, inflexibility, and intolerance are the raw manifestations of pride, but these are overwhelmed by the accommodation, charity, faith, approachability, hope, and sociability of the repentant.

As we
repent, we
draw upon the
magnificent power
of all three members
of the Godhead, so that
we may become increasingly
receptive to flashes of insight;
to be cast off into streams of
revelation that carry us along
in the quickening currents of
direct experience with our
Heavenly Father, with
Jesus Christ and
with the Holy
Ghost.

Every day,
we make the
choice to repent
or not to repent,
with decisions that
we pray to God will
be illuminated and
reinforced by our
principles.

When
Adam and
Eve were driven
from the Garden,
they were "punished"
with the very thing that
would later prove to bring
them the greatest happiness. As
the Sufi poet Rumi observed, our
wounds become portals that allow
light to enter us. A Savior would be
provided for them, but in the interim,
cherubim and a flaming sword were
placed to keep the way of the Tree
of Life, to honor the doctrines of
Justice and Mercy, as well as
the principle of repentance,
that they had been taught
in consequence of their
transgression.

Following
repentance, we
may remember our
sins, but only in the
sense that they increase
our testimonies. Because there
must needs be opposition in all
things, our Father in Heaven uses
sin (and repentance) to strengthen
us to be more stalwart soldiers
in the army of Christ. In this
way, sin may work to His,
and even to our,
advantage.

Repentance
can be a difficult
road to negotiate, but it
brings about lasting change.
It requires great courage, much
strength, many tears, unceasing
prayers, and untiring efforts.
It is hard work, but the
retirement benefits
are out of this
world.

Within our busy and complex world, we often see through a glass darkly, making it very difficult for us to know how to harness the power of the elusive equations found within the awesome principle of repentance.

The
Haz-Mat Protocol
of repentance has been
written into The Plan to
detoxify us from the cares
and conditioning influences
of the world, and from the
homogenization process
that occurs as we are
worn down by the
vicissitudes
of life.

The brilliantly crafted principle of repentance has been designed as a celestial thermostat that easily mitigates the intensity of the telestial tempests that so regularly sweep across the landscapes of our lives.

Heavenly Father
knows us quite well,
and has taken care to
provide for our welfare,
as we shoot the rapids of
life. It is only the life jacket
of repentance that can help us
to keep our heads above water
as we struggle for air in the
turbulence of telestial
torrents.

Disciples of Christ who
repent would not dream
of postponing enrollment in
a curriculum patterned after
heaven, nor would they defer
their Gospel-oriented studies
in favor of worldly pursuits
that ask for pitifully little
in terms of commitment
or effort, and that
offer very little
in terms of
reward.

Those who
worship idols
of any kind are
blinded to the reality
that their faith is flawed,
and that the objects of their
desires do not have the power
to deliver on any of their
promises, much less the
power to save.

The guilt
and pain of
unresolved sin
can feel like an
unquenchable fire
that leaves our hope
for happiness in ashes.
In so many ways, our
repentance teaches us
about the spirit of
reconciliation.

We who
desire forgiveness
must learn that we may
not hold anything back. It
is necessary to invest everything
we have, including our assurance,
anticipation, confidence, conviction,
expectation, and trust in the power
of the Atonement to deliver on
its almost incomprehensible
promise that it can save
us from our sins.

When
we are
offended or
perceive that we
have been hurt by
others, or are injured
physically, intellectually,
emotionally, professionally,
or even spiritually, we need
the balm of our benevolent
blindness to soothe
the trauma.

We cannot
allow the better
angels of our nature
to be overcome by our
eagerness, or waste our
efforts and squander our
precious resources in
the conceptual cul-
de-sacs of life.

Those who have brushed up against the face of death often describe their "out of body" experience. Members of the Lord's Church feel the same when they have been redeemed from spiritual death; when they "walk in newness of life." (Romans 6:4).

The
Apostle
Paul echoed
the teaching of
Nephi, writing that
it is by grace that we
are saved, through faith,
and that not of ourselves.
"It is the gift of God."
(Ephesians 2:8).

Repentance
figuratively paints
the portrait of a turtle
on a fence post. When we
repent, we know one thing
for certain. That turtle
had help getting
up there.

We never
forget that it
was the restoration
of truth that realigned
religious practice with the
eternal principle of repentance.
The Church was restored lest we be
spoiled "through philosophy and vain
deceit, after the tradition of men,
after the rudiments of the world,
and not after Christ."
(Colossians 2:8).

When the new
clothes we are wearing
when we go out to play on
terra firma become soiled by
our interaction with sin, because
of repentance we can forsake our
filthiness in favor of clean heavenly
vestments. Unlike the imaginary outfit
that was made by duplicitous tailors for
the Emperor in the fable by Hans Christian
Anderson, the celestial garments we wear
are tangible; they are real. We need not
fear the cries of children in the streets
who shout: "But they aren't wearing
anything at all!"

God's Plan
of Repentance
and Mercy smooths
out the bumps on our
ride through mortality,
and gives our experiences
a profoundly positive twist,
energizing them with vitality
and us with the capacity to
re-write the last chapters
of our life-story; even
to alter eternity.

The Savior
taught us to be
patient, even in the
face of challenges when
our portion seems unfair,
when our difficulties seem
unreasonable, and when
the proportions of the
problems looming
before us seem
daunting.

Our failure to repent is a form of rebellion against our Heavenly Father. As was the case following the insurgency of Lucifer, there need to be consequences, though they may be eternally damaging in their scope.

When we do
not repent, the
Holy Spirit, which
burns like a fire, will
be quenched, and the
Atonement will lose
its power to save
us from our
sins.

We will be unclean in the sight of God, as long as we remain incapable of maintaining undeviating obedience to celestial principles.

Heaven always
holds its breath while
waiting upon the initiative
of those who are charged with
the responsibility to provide a
good example, and to take
the lead when it comes
to repentance.

Death is the
Golden Ticket
that reintroduces us
to the secret garden of
our primeval childhood,
and to the wonders of
eternity that lie in
wait for us just
beyond its
gate.

We
are slow
to mischief when
we exercise our ability
to look past our telestial
temptations and temporal
trivia; when we possess the
will to adjust our perspective
so that the achievement of
righteous goals becomes
our obsession.

Spiritual neglect
requires drastic action. The
plastic surgery of repentance is
indicated if we hope to experience
a reversal of our fortunes and if
we hope to reflect the likeness
and image of God in our
countenances.

Faith is dead, without the accompanying work of repentance that is made possible by the Atonement. Even great faith lacks the power to save us from the unalterable demands of Justice. So that Mercy might prevail, God provided us with a Mediator.

Without
the Lord's spiritual
fitness program that was
designed to help us achieve
symmetry through repentance,
day-to-day life in the lone
and dreary world would
lack coherence and
stability.

Those who refuse to repent have hard hearts, stiff-necks, and are overtly and covertly rebellious. They lack the malleability and the pliability of those who are humbly repentant.

Because
we faithfully
persist in the process
of repentance, the Spirit
will teach us how to become
engaged in fashioning defensive
weapons in our armory of thought.
It is with these tools that the Lord
will show us just how we will be
able to construct the heavenly
fortifications of love, joy,
strength, and peace.

Alma taught that in the absence of repentance for their sins, and without the benefit of covenants, Adam and Eve would have ultimately been miserable. To be certain, they would have lived forever, but it would have been in an unrelenting state of alienation from the presence of God.

There is an
ever-present
negative energy
that can influence
our affairs, and the
Atonement is its only
viable countermeasure.
Its sole stipulations are
that we confess when we
have, in any magnitude,
embraced the opposites
that lie before us, and
that we immediately
undertake the safety
protocols required
by repentance to
orient us once
again toward
our home in
heaven.

Repentance
means forsaking
the carnal nature
that is nothing more
than a shadowy after
image of Lucifer's
rebellion at the
Council.

Some eagerly take up
the sword of vengeance as
if it were somehow their God-
given right and responsibility. In
contrast to those who use religion
to legitimize vindictive behavior, we
believe that the Savior must surely
smile upon simple expressions
and acts of charity that are
much more effective at
paving the way to
reconciliation
with others.

Our
exercise
of free will in
an atmosphere of
opposition propels us
onward toward immortality
and eternal life, as long as we
rely upon ordinances, covenants,
and the Atonement of Christ
to keep the sand of sin
out of our gears.

Repentance allows us to make mistakes, to learn from them, and to then grasp the horns of sanctuary so that at the end of the day we may still be justified by the grace of God.

No matter
that we may, for all
intents and purposes, be
dead weight, the Savior has
the strength to carry us until
we have been revitalized, and
can once again walk and
not be weary, and run
and not faint.

The Atonement anticipated the shortcomings, the sins of omission, and the sins of commission that would be frustratingly, repetitively, and painfully committed by men and women, and boys and girls, from the very beginning to the end of time.

The principle of
repentance provides
us with currency sufficient
for our needs, but it also allows
us, if we choose to do so, to substitute
its legal tender for wads of counterfeit
cash with which late payments may be
made with interest and penalties
tacked on for bad behavior.

As an integral
part of the process
of repentance, it is our
benevolent blindness to
overlook the faults of
others that molds us
in ways that no
other quality
can.

Our
benevolent
blindness, and that
of our Heavenly Father
Who is quick to forgive His
repentant children, may very
well be the one sense that
can unerringly guide us
back to the lucidity
and brilliant light
our eternal
Home.

It is by grace that
our burdens are lightened
when we find them too heavy
to bear alone. Then it stands
ready to pluck us out of the
gaping jaws of hell, and
whisk us out of harm's
way right into the
embrace of
God.

Repentance
is a catalyst
that releases the
powers of Heaven
in our behalf.

When we find
that we have become
unwilling passengers on
an emotional roller coaster,
we realize that it is driven, in
part, "in consequence of evils and
designs which do and will exist
in the hearts of conspiring
men in the last days."
(D&C 89:4).

Repentance
reassures us to know
that although "the stars fade
away, and the sun himself grow
dim with age and nature sink in
years, we shall flourish in immortal
youth, unhurt amidst the war of
elements, the wreck of matter,
and the crash of worlds."
(Joseph Addison).

When we repent,
we recognize and act
upon moments when the
Spirit leads us to recall
President Kimball's caution.
"Seeking the spectacular," he
said, "we sometimes miss the
constant flow of revealed
communication that
comes."

As we minister among our fellow travelers, we understand the wisdom of the Savior's statement that "whosoever will save his life shall lose it. But whosoever will lose his life for my sake, the same shall save it." (Luke 9:24).

Paul's formula for ridding ourselves of excess baggage was "forgetting those things which are behind (us), and reaching unto those things which are before" us. (Philippians 3:13). All good things come to those who wait.

Choice is
at the heart
of the Gospel
of Jesus Christ,
and repentance
nudges us off our
comfortable cushions
of complacency, setting
us squarely on the hot
seat of our personal
accountability.

Traveling along the road of repentance in the direction of forgiveness may take some time, and in the short term, there may be reverses. But over the long haul, as we move to higher plateaus, God's Plan will be there. In times of discouragement, we remember the observation of James: "We count them happy which endure." (James 5:11).

When we present ourselves before God, because of the Atonement, we will be uncompromised by corruption.

God's pattern provides us with many opportunities during mortality for repentance, so that we might put our fingers to the pulse of discipleship as we test the promises of guiding principles. Once again, the elegant simplicity of Heavenly Father's Plan trumps the deception, confusion, and complexity of its convoluted and confusing counterfeits.

Satan grossly
misjudged the ability of the
Redeemer of the world to save
all mankind thru the Atonement.
As it turned out, all that would be
necessary to restore our purity was
the further light and knowledge
that He had promised to give
us. Satan never saw that
one coming.

When things seem too good to be true, by the power of the Holy Ghost each of us may discern if they be so, or not.

As the gates of
baptism swing open
to reveal a strait and
narrow way before us that
stretches away to a glow of
light on the eastern horizon,
our real journey to Christ
has only just begun.

Repentance
forgets about
what is absent and
instead concentrates
on what is available.
It does not allow
what is missing
to paralyze or
defeat
us.

Under the best of circumstances, both in and out of the Church, "we talk of Christ, we rejoice in Christ, we preach of Christ, we prophesy of Christ, and we write according to our prophecies, that our children may know to what source they may look for a remission of their sins." (2 Nephi 25:26).

We outlast
and counteract
negative influences
by doing everything we
can to be positive. Unless
we endure in righteousness,
we cannot be saved from the
self-defeating behaviors
that eat away at our
foundation.

The
Atonement
of Christ charges
us to look up to God
before we take a leap of
faith. (See D&C 42:51).
The Savior invites us
to repent, and to
do it now.

When repentance has
stretched and molded us,
its expression will be manifest
in an unblemished and alabaster
skin-tone. We will have the look
of those who have been born
again to a newness
of life.

When
the barrier
protection of
repentance shields
our divine center, the
prospect of our return
to the full stature of
our spirits is all but
guaranteed.

We have all
witnessed those
who have vacationed
in Idumea to celebrate
the festival of free will and
the carnival of carefree living.
But we also remember Paul, who
shed his telestial trappings, that
he might experience a greater
comprehension of
eternity.

The trouble
with vanity is
that it relies on
false hope and its
strength is built upon
false premises. It is a
Ponzi scheme that cannot
deliver on its promises. It
writes checks that cannot
be cashed because it has
no spiritual reserves. It
is forever teetering
on the brink of
bankruptcy.

After Alice had
fallen down the rabbit
hole, she met the Cheshire Cat,
and asked him: "Would you please tell
me which way I ought to go from here?"
To which the cat responded: "That depends
a good deal on where you want to go." Alice
acknowledged: "I admit, I don't much care
where." The cat rejoined: "Then it really
doesn't matter which way you go." Alice
implored: "Just so I go somewhere!"
To which the cat observed: "Oh,
you are sure to do that, if
you only walk far
enough."

When we give in to temptation and consciously do the wrong thing, we are enticed by the lowest common denominator in the mathematical equations that will, sooner or later, define our character.

Benevolent blindness is not spiritual myopia, but rather is a catalyst that can trigger visual acuity reaching out to an eternal perspective.

Forgiveness
thru repentance
is a gift, and is a
manifestation of the
grace of God. It was
conceived to reconfigure
carnality into celestial
certainty and elevate
us to exaltation.

One of the
basic messages
of the Restoration
is that Adam and Eve
fell that they might have
joy while on earth, as well
as in heaven, thru repentance
that had been activated by
their faith in the power
of the Atonement.

Those who
endure to the
end must avoid
embracing idea-gods
that would otherwise rivet
their attention, consume their
energies, demand their devotion,
divert their direction, obscure their
objectivity, and dilute their God
given capacity to make positive
changes thru repentance.

We do not write
checks that cannot be
cashed. More importantly,
neither does the Savior. He
has limitless reserves in His
bank account, and He has
given us his P.I.N., made
up entirely of letters:
R.e.p.e.n.t.a.n.c.e.
Let him see
Who has
eyes.

If mortality
could be visualized in
spatial dimensions, it would
take the shape of an hourglass,
with the strait gate represented by
its narrow midsection. After passing
through that constriction following
an exercise of faith and purposeful
repentance, amazing vistas would
open up to reveal to our eyes
unparalleled opportunity.

Repentance
grounds us to
practical belief, but
its elements commit us
to an upward thrust.
It confirms that
we are known
to God.

Because
of repentance,
the Law of Mercy
trumps the immutable
Law of Justice through
forgiveness because
of the Atonement.

The Atonement looks directly into the jaws of spiritual death without averting its eyes. It was not the Savior, but the Devil who was the first to blink as he was unceremoniously cast out of heaven, a fallen son of the morning!

After the Fall,
the portal to Eden
may have swung shut,
but as it did so, another
door opened that introduced
Adam and Eve to a secret garden
accessible only to those who would
utilize the power of the Atonement.
By obedience to the principles of
The Plan, they would experience
both good and evil, pleasure
and pain, as well as light
and darkness, in the
white hot crucible
of experience.

A puckish
observation
is that revenge
is a dish that is best
served cold, when we are
no longer caught up in the
heat of the moment, but think
that we can afford to be crafty,
cunning, and calculating as we plot
our payback. But that strategy is like
swallowing poison and hoping it will
kill the other guy. Our repentance,
and the Savior's forgiveness,
don't work that
way.

Repentance is
just the prescription
the Doctor ordered to
treat the religious fever
that elevates our testimony
temperature enough to get
our juices flowing with
an appreciation of the
Savior's sacrifice.

Recurring repentance teaches us to suppress the natural inclinations of the telestial world that surround us, continually encroaching upon our spiritual stability, and threatening to erode our faith and testimony of the principles of the Gospel.

Repentance relentlessly drives us forward with an unwavering confidence that God's power to save will be unleashed in our behalf and flow over our wounds as a healing balm.

The
unrepentant are
argumentative; they
abuse their position and
exercise unrighteous dominion,
while the humble speak softly, seek
peaceful solutions, invite the Spirit to
guide them in their interpersonal
relationships, and acknowledge
their love of God and man
as the engine that drives
their behavior.

It is our
honesty with ourselves
that tests the mettle of
our convictions. Through
our repentance, we put our
money where our mouth is. We
have no proof until we act on
the basis of trust. Then, comes
the confirmation of the reality
as feelings of self-confidence
grow and purposeful actions
replace tentative overtures.
In effect, we let go
and let God.

The Atonement allows us to overcome our selfishness and our indefensible desire for Mercy without Justice. But this is nothing more than a doctrine of the devil.

The cataracts that are created by our concessions to sin cloud our vision. Our narrow perspective forces us into making comfortless compromises, leaving the landscapes of our lives as nothing more than empty shells. If we do not take advantage of the therapy of repentance, the prognosis is poor for eyes that have lost the ability to see clearly, and that can no longer make the distinctions between good and evil, and between light and darkness.

It
is in
the House
of the Lord
that we see how
the Atonement can
become both infinite
and eternal in
its scope.

Repentance
is a constructive
process that has been
designed to build us up,
even if it has to first tear
us down. It is involved with
recovery, to be sure. But
its primary focus is
on discovery.

When we repent, we are better able to recognize the truth that we are beings of light who are enjoying the experience of mortality.

When we are assaulted
by sounding brass and tinkling
cymbals, those with a strong testimony
of the gift of repentance will find within
the Atonement the ability to sift through
a discordant cacophony of confusing
voices to find revealed truth.

Our repentance is completed as soon as the Spirit of the Lord has fallen upon us, and we are filled with joy. When we are clean, we enjoy a peace of conscience that defies any explanation.

A desired result of all Gospel-oriented teaching is achieved when a mighty change has been wrought in our hearts and we have no more disposition to do evil, but to continually do good.

When we
acquire a taste
for the poor imitations
of life that are peddled by the
deceiver, we delude ourselves into
believing they are the genuine articles.
We assuage ourselves with rationalizations
so we can face ourselves in the mirror, and
sleep better. The irony is that in other and more
productive circumstances, our consciences might
have been tormented by our own demons as our
delusions unfolded before us. The forgery
might thereby have been revealed by the
the light and the life of the world,
prompting us to speedily repent,
as if the welfare of our
souls depended
on it.

Because
repentance
sees stepping
stones instead of
stumbling blocks, even
negative experiences and
the crises of confidence
can be transformed into
opportunities that have
favorable outcomes
to be savored.

Those who repent,
seek divine direction,
and learn how to focus
the powers of heaven in their
behalf. They take advantage of
the Savior's invitation to be cast off
into a stream of revelation and to be
carried along in quickening currents
of experience with the Holy Ghost,
Who justifies their efforts to
improve their nature.

1,449
of the verses
in The Book of
Mormon state a life
preserving truth: "It came
to pass." It did not come to
stay! Life unfolds before our
eyes, often in surprisingly
delightful ways. Our
repentance helps
us to weather
the storms.

Our performance requirements focus solely upon the principles and ordinances of the Gospel. "Whosoever repenteth and cometh unto me," said the Lord, "the same is my Church. Whosoever declareth more or less than this, the same is not of me, but is against me. Therefore, he is not of my Church." (D&C 10:67-68).

The Atonement has such power that even if we have been wounded by our sins, they will not heal imperfectly as soul-scars. Any evidence that there has ever been telestial trauma will disappear with the application of the Balm of Gilead.

It is
our heartfelt
repentance that
helps us to redefine
and redesign what had
heretofore been stumbling
blocks; they are repurposed
into the very stepping stones
that are needed to conquer
our fears, to reinforce our
confidence, and overcome
the obstacles that are
strewn about along
the path of our
progression.

It is nothing short of sin that motivates us to drag our battered and beaten bodies to the local chapter of Weight Watchers, known as The Church of Jesus Christ of Latter-day Saints.

Angels will attend us as we repent: "For I will go before your face," promised the Lord. "I will be on your right hand, and on your left, and my Spirit shall be in your hearts, and mine angels round about you, to bear you up." (D&C 84:88). With such a promise, how could we think to turn our backs on such reinforcement, return to our wicked ways, and go it alone?

Without redemption from sin, if they were to have partaken of the fruit of the Tree of Life, which is eternal life, or the highest expression of the love of God, it would not have been possible for Adam and Eve to sustain a celestial existence, inasmuch as in their current condition they would have been incapable of obedience to the laws that govern those who merit a heavenly glory. Thereby, the Plan of Salvation would have been frustrated for all of the children of God.

We cannot superficially whitewash our sins to cover them up, no matter how hard we try.

Our
purpose in
life is to grow in
grace, that we might
progress in stature until
we reach the point that we
have developed both the
image and likeness
of our Heavenly
Father.

The gifts of God expand our vision, that we might embrace an appreciation of principles that relate to the eternities.

Regarding sins for
which we have repented,
we will remember them only
insofar as they intensify our
testimonies and strengthen our
resolve to refrain from repeating
them, but we will no longer feel
the guilt associated with
the transgression.

The quality
of forgiveness
is really a celestial
barometer, calibrated
to a scale that measures
the capacity of our hearts.

In the Gospel Plan,
our repentance constitutes
the principal of the principle
of forgiveness. In the prescribed
process of receiving a remission of
our sins, we discover the tangible
evidence of "a better and an
enduring substance."
(Hebrews 10:34).

When
the repentant
are pure in heart,
they enjoy the intrinsic
countermeasures to wicked
imaginations. Their behavior is
driven by altruism, self-denial,
self-discipline, self-restraint,
and self-sacrifice; these all
come as we listen with our
hearts to the promptings
of the Spirit that come
to us as a gentle
breeze.

Sometimes
all too quickly,
and sometimes agonizingly
slowly, those who have sold their
souls to the Devil for a mess of pottage
are dragged down to a hell on earth that
is of their own construction. Their bad habits
are the result of repetitively impulsive behaviors
that, in a rising tide of wickedness, continually
erode away at the foundations of agency.
They are fettered by the chains of their
compulsions. Too late, they
realize that unlimited
freedom leads to
tyranny.

The
baubles
of Babylon
are a bribery;
they are brazen
opposites of the
incorruptible
riches of
eternity.

Those of weak
will who voluntarily
or involuntarily give up
their agency in exchange for
whatever provocative pleasures
their poor choices may provide, are
snared by Satan and bound by his strong
chains. Too late, they realize that their
misguided loyalties have fettered
their self expression, limited
their options, and have
restricted their
actions.

Our faith impels us to action. When we follow up on our righteous impressions, it is as though we have enjoyed God's perfect understanding. We have knowledge, after all.

The Atonement is the only fire retardant that can be dumped on the raging inferno of sin.

No
wind can
blow except
it fills our sails to
carry each of us ever
closer to our destination,
without delay or interruption,
and without unnecessary cost,
loss, or sacrifice. All that is
required is the sacrifice of
our broken hearts and
contrite spirits.

Yielding to the enticements of Satan leaves us gasping for a breath of celestial air.

When we sling
mud, we lose ground.
If we hope to successfully
deal with the inequalities of
life and escape the quicksands
of self-pity, we must personalize
the lessons of the Atonement.
We must change our nature
to become new creatures
in Christ, light on our
feet, and quick to
respond to His
counsel.

God knows
what is best and
He has confidence
in our divine potential
to develop His nature. He
commands us to repent, to be
baptized, and to develop perfect
faith. Because these realistic goals
are easily within the reach of all
of His children, they become the
basic requirements for those
who hope to one day gain
readmittance to His
Kingdom.

The Devil urges us to follow a detour from the strait and narrow way, that leads only through telestial traffic, conceptual cul-de-sacs, religious roundabout, and doctrinal dead ends, from which escape is only possible with repentance.

The
Plan provides
the means to reset
our spiritual appestat
when we notice it is out
of whack, and we find
ourselves indulging,
and even binge
eating, in
sin.

The Atonement has purpose and meaning only for those who are willing to sacrifice their broken heart and contrite spirit to the Savior of the world.

Because
of our exercise
of free will that is
always carried out in
an atmosphere of opposition,
undesirable consequences are
likely to follow. Their effects
can only be mitigated by
repentance.

Repentance
is nurtured within
the rich culture medium
of faith, validated by baptism
in a metaphysical reunion with
God. It is witnessed in the fiery
cauldron of the Spirit, in the
only way that is possible,
to ransom us from
our sins.

Weakness
can seed the
atmosphere of
our inspiration, to
nurture and moisten
our tender testimonies
as well as to germinate
our budding desire to
repent of our wicked
ways.

It is
our faith,
the companion
of repentance, that
motivates us to action
by jarring us out of
our complacency
toward our
standing
before
God.

Repentance
sets us free to
be creative, and
sets us creative to
become more free, by
unleashing the doctrine
of the kingdom and
releasing it so it
can work its
magic.

The reach of the Lord's sacrifice extends so far that it has power to neutralize the sins of the best of us and the worst of us; it is infinite in both its temporal and eternal influence, and it only waits upon our initiative to manifest its dynamic energy.

Repentance has the
divine potential to order
our chaotic world, to bless us
with clarity rather than confusion,
to teach us fluency in the language
of the Spirit, and to educate those
who are functionally illiterate, so
that all might be mesmerized
by the power of the Word.

Forgiveness of sin stands at attention before the golden gate of heaven, patiently waiting for us to recognize the power of the Atonement to transform our lives.

Those who refuse to repent have forsaken their core values, and succumb to an obsession for things that can never satisfy their voracious appetites.

When
pride swells
in our bosom, it
takes up a volume
that squeezes out
the capacity for
real heart-felt
repentance
on our
part.

Faith is not
to have a perfect
knowledge of things
gained through our own
experience. Misguided trust
in temporal trivia may seem
to be a logical approach, but
it is the enemy of faith because
it befriends procrastination as
it ignorantly rationalizes our
failure to speedily repent
of all our sins.

If we
do not reach
out to grasp the
horns of sanctuary,
we deny the invitation
of God to throw ourselves
upon His mercy seat. Our
inaction compromises
the solidarity of
our spirits.

We need to
repent so that the
lingering effects of its
afterglow is so compelling
that it overshadows any latent
images of our former reflection
in the windows of even the
tallest telestial
towers.

There is a
visibly different look to
those who have repented, taken
their vows, and have moved upward
in the direction of higher plateaus that
become launchpads for affirmative action.
Their features are flushed with confidence.
They stand out from the crowd. They are
enthusiastic, passionate, fervent, eager,
animated, excited by life, and get a
high from the natural release of
the endorphins that flood
their systems with
excitement.

Grace has the
power to raise us
up from physical death
by the Resurrection, and
from spiritual death thru the
Atonement of Christ. We receive
the grace of God proportionately
as we conform to His standard
of personal righteousness
that is required by
the Gospel.

Those who
enjoy the fruits
of faith and the spirit
of repentance maintain an
unshakeable conviction that we
are the sons and daughters of
God with promises to keep
and miles to go before
we sleep.

"Gather the people together, men, and women, and children, and the stranger that is within thy gates, that they may hear, and that they may learn, and fear the Lord your God, and observe to do all the words of this law." (Deuteronomy 31:12).

Job encouraged us to "forget (our) misery, and remember it as waters that pass away." (Job 11:16). Difficulty in times past is water that is under the bridge.

Repentance
concentrates on
available resources,
and harnesses them with
the power of the Atonement.
It molds them into forces for
positive, substantial, and
significant change.

The children of men can be transformed by grace into sons and daughters of God.

The marvel of God's love is that the more we attempt to serve Him, the more He blesses us. Thereby, we become even more deeply indebted to Him, and we remain so forever. When we are redeemed by the blood of Christ, it will be by His grace alone that we experience salvation.

The repentant faithful remind us of Abinadi, of whom the scriptures record: "The Spirit of the Lord was upon him and his face shone with exceeding luster." (Mosiah 13:5). They stand out, and are in sharp contrast to the unrepentant, whose sullen and downcast eyes betray the fact that they have become mired in sin and are bound by iniquity.

Repentance
gives us repetitive
opportunities to practice
jumping out of our telestial
skin, off of our complacency
plateaus, into more comfortable,
form-fitting, celestial silhouettes
that empower us to leap tall
buildings in a single
bound.

People think
that they can be
happy if they wander
and play, forgetting that
a key feature of The Plan
is to ponder and pray, which
thing leads them to appreciate
the Atonement, and to speedily
repent of their sins. Only then
will they find the happiness
that has been prepared
for the Saints.

When we repent,
our Father gives us
the opportunity to be
repetitively re-vitalized,
as we are re-introduced
to a Magical Kingdom
where our hopes and
our dreams really
do come true.

Our
Lord Jesus
Christ taught
that we must be
perfect, for otherwise
we cannot hope to inherit
the Kingdom of God. Perhaps
He meant that we must be
quick to repent of all
of our sins.

With the
the Atonement,
the elements of The
Plan that, at first blush,
seemed to stand in opposition
to life have become the pathway
and portal to a joyful reunion
in the eternities, where we will
meet our families before the
pleasing bar of God.

Perfect repentance, that is witnessed by the Spirit of Justification, compels us to consider the possibility that, one day, we might actually be holy and without spot, as is our Lord and Savior.

The opposite of the
path to Calvary is the road to
self-indulgence; the opposite of
submission to the will of God is
self-gratification, and the
opposite of reverential
worship is idolatry.
It is that plain
and simple.

Lucifer fell from heaven with a deafening thud. We feel its after-shock even today, as our knees shake under the weight of sin.

The insolvency of Satan's seduction cannot be mitigated by a third-party bailout. The only solution to his nepotism is to repent.

Repentance brings us into harmony with the eternities. It helps us to overcome the world with a freedom from confinement to the inexorable immutability of the destructive laws that govern our temporal world.

Our faith
notwithstanding,
we are saved by the
grace of God, after all
we can do, and that
is primarily to
repent.

When we have repented, we are in harmony with God's purpose and His Spirit envelops our lives in ways that are almost sacramental in their scope and in their effect upon our future.

The principle of repentance gives us enough rope to either hang ourselves, or to lasso the stars and hitch our wagons to eternity.

We are
benevolently
blind when we
differentiate between
persons and their behavior,
when we see only the acorns
of mighty oaks in the character
of others who may be struggling to
germinate a basic understanding
of core principles, and when we
look beyond performance and
see only potential.

Often, when we repent,
the Spirit compels us to jump
from the frying pan right into the
fire. With practice, however, when we
make that leap of faith, we will land
on springboards to action that will
vault us upward toward safety,
so that we might balance with
confidence on pinnacles of
perfection throughout the
remaining scenes of the
second Act of the
Three Act
Play.

In everything, we give thanks, for God has made promises to us "with an immutable covenant that they shall be fulfilled, and all things wherewith (we) have been afflicted shall work together for our good." (D&C 98:3). For our own part, "the woods are lovely, dark, and deep. But we have promises to keep, and miles to go before we sleep." (Robert Frost).

Actively
relying upon
the power of the
Atonement can be a
strong generator
of positive
energy.

If we allow
ourselves to sink
into the quicksand of
carnality, and we lose the
wide-eyed innocence of youth,
our purity, and our holiness, we
forfeit the happiness that can
only accompany untroubled
souls through the miracle
of the Atonement of
the Redeemer of
the world.

Satan grooms
his willing disciples
to engage in a twisted
reasoning that encourages
them to rationalize their quest
for the holy grail of power, wealth,
dominion, position, and influence.
But these are poor substitutes for
humility, meekness, modesty,
restraint, repentance, and
happiness; these are the
real cornerstones
of provident
living.

The influence of the Light of Christ encourages us to fix our sights on the pole-star of repentance, that has been designed to lift us to higher plateaus of personal progress. Work we must, but our lunch is free, provided by the Savior of the world.

In addition
to forgiveness
for our sins, one
of the blessings of
repentance is that we
will receive the strength
to endure the suffering
that is part of life, but
that is not of our
own making.

If we repent, the way is paved for our Father to be both just and merciful at the same time; all because of the Atonement.

Repentance
provides a way
for us to increase our
metaphysical metabolism,
to burn away as much of the
fat of faithlessness as we can,
when our hearts are broken
in the fiery hot crucible
of contrition.

In the
Atonement,
our innate desire
to be clean finds its
expression in celestial
sparks that ignite our
desire to repent.

In a classic
demonstration of His
magnificent omniscience,
Our Father in Heaven negotiated
with Justice from a position of power,
because He had beforehand conceived
the Atonement, in order to make
possible our metamorphosis
from imperfect children
to beings of light.

The Atonement may be hard for us to grasp because it was conceived in heaven. It is not of this world, and so if we try to wrap our finite minds around it, we will fail to do so. It is spiritually discerned.

We are the acorns
of a mighty oak. Our
testimony of the principle
of repentance motivates us,
uplifts us, and inspires us
to reconnect with our
intrinsic nobility.

The Lord recognizes that even the righteous do not become perfect overnight. Therefore, He has promised: "As often as my people repent will I forgive them their trespasses." (Mosiah 26:30).

At its core, the doctrine of Christ becomes a perfectly liberating law that allows us to reach our potential in a mutually supportive atmosphere of inter-dependency with the Savior.

Repentance is like a
chiropractic adjustment
to treat spiritual scoliosis.
It heals us, that we might be
strong and healthy enough
to bear the crosses of
the world without a
single word of
complaint.

As we are
carried along and
enveloped by the Spirit
during the course of our
repentance, we feel the
influence of the Lord
God as if it were an
all-consuming fire
in our bones.

Of ourselves, we lack the power to start over and make a new beginning, but with repentance, we can begin to create a new ending. With the help of our Savior, we can rewrite our life's story. In truth, they are fairytales that are simply waiting to be written by the finger of God.

The blessings of human decency, concern, and brotherly kindness are part of the severance package that we accepted when we elected to sustain The Plan of Salvation and committed to leave our home in heaven to enjoy our turn on earth.

If we
just don't
care, we are
likely to wind
up with a bucket
full of chokeberries,
instead of the plump
huckleberries that
we intended to
harvest in
life.

If we so happen
to be startled by the
corruptible reflection we
see as we pass by the windows
of a great and spacious building,
we need to repent without hesitation,
remembering that "the Lord seeth not
as man seeth; for man looketh on
the outward appearance, but the
Lord looketh on the heart."
(1 Samuel 16:7).

Because of our
repentance, the grass really
is greener on the other side of
the pasture. Its pleasant pastoral
environment extends the promise
of a refreshingly new perspective
on life that follows the strait
and narrow way past the
principle of repentance
all the way to the
greenhouse of
the Lord.

God allows us to grow until we have been sanctified and justified "through the grace of our Lord and Savior Jesus Christ." (D&C 20:30-32). It is in this sense that Nephi declared that we are saved by grace only after all we can do, which is primarily to repent of all of our sins.

We are at
risk of falling
into transgression
in consequence of our
shallow understanding of
the principle of repentance.
As Alma declared to the people
of Ammonihah, "The scriptures are
before you. If ye will wrest them it
shall be to your own destruction."
(Alma 13:20). Picking apart the
word of God distorts dogma
into meaningless fragments
without any coherent
connection.

We are
converted
to the concept
of repentance when
we begin to hear it as
it calls to us, inviting us
to come in out of the cold;
out of the darkness into
the marvelous Light
of day.

Repentance
endows us with
the power to reach
out to touch the face of
God with an incorruptible
and unassailable spiritual
sixth sense that finds its
expression deep inside
us, within our own
hearts.

Our
progression
hinges upon the
the principles of the
Atonement, repentance,
and forgiveness, which are
the opposites of damnation,
condemnation, and life
without light.

Conduct that is sinful might look fashionable to some, but the styles that are popular today can change ever so quickly.

To appreciate
just how thoughtfully
the principle of repentance
was conceived, we need to go
back to the inventive period when
matter was organized, the elements
were brought into harmony out of
chaos, and a beautiful Garden
was created eastward
in Eden.

Only with repentance does mortality become the wonderful center for the talented and gifted that was envisioned by our Father.

If we
do not beg for
our own forgiveness,
and if we do not forgive
those who have purportedly
trespassed against us, we will
find ourselves in a spiritual
vacuum, gasping for life
sustaining air while we
are only inches away
from rescue.

The Devil's bribery stands in sharp contrast and in opposition to the blessings that follow our repentance.

Through the Atonement, we may receive the kinds of immortal bodies that we will need in the resurrection, if we hope to thrive in celestial fire.

Repentance
is the catalyst
that propels us
upward toward the
discovery of personal
levels of experience
with the Savior.

When we
have repented,
we have no more
disposition to do
evil, but to do
continually
do good.

Our own
forgiveness can
act as a pacemaker,
doling out therapeutic
pulses of doctrinal energy
to those who need it
the most.

The Plan of our
Father envisions a
Utopian society, but it
also provides repentance
as a practical solution for
those whose agency has
led them away from
the Rod of Iron.

As long as
we have donned the
life vest of repentance,
and it remains securely in
place, we will be prepared to
deal with whatever challenges
the rapids of life might choose
to cast our way. High water can
even be our friend, as it carries
us down life's river over the
boulders, logs, and ledges
that are the figurative
obstacles to our
progression.

God's Plan
rests on solid
footings that are
reinforced with the
rebar of repentance.
The Stone of Israel
is our foundation.

Of the
confused,
abandoned,
and disillusioned
disciples of Satan who
lie strewn in his wake, who
wander the boulevards of the
twin cities of worldliness and
pleasure, the Savior said: "They
seek not the Lord to establish
his righteousness" through
purposeful repentance.
(D&C 1:16).

The world's exaggerations stretch our comprehension and credulity, causing us to stand unsteadily on our spiritual tippy-toes, as we roll the dice and leave our destiny in the hands of lady luck.

We can do nothing that puts God in our debt. His grace is completely beyond our ability to pay. But He never demands that we settle our account with Him; He only asks that we keep His commandments.

We are
accountable
for our own actions,
which will either destroy us
or, through the Atonement, lift
us into the embrace of angels. We
cannot have it both ways. If we sow
sparingly, we shall reap sparingly,
and if we sow bountifully we
shall also reap bountifully.
(See 2 Corinthians 9:6).

The
beauty of
repentance is that
it can be a primer on
midwifery, with the Savior
our labor coach, as we begin
the arduous birthing process
of our reunion with God
that we characterize
as being born
again.

Unless our behavior is in harmony with the laws of the Gospel, unrestrained freedom must inevitably lead to a crushing tyranny.

Those who
repent have learned
how to identify, and to
deal with, the hidden costs
of self-indulgence. They take
care that they do not indebt
themselves to the usurious
interest rate that is
levied by the
Devil.

When our
quest to be
clean in the
sight of God
is approached
casually, we are
as vain imposters.

Those who refuse Heavenly Father's invitation to repent seek refuge in the fortress of their own accomplishments. In order to maintain outward appearances, the hasty fabrication of a façade is required that demands inordinate attention to trivial detail as well as continual cosmetic reconstruction. "What a tangled web we weave, when first we practice to deceive" (Sir Walter Scott).

By faith,
we partake
of the divine
nature, with the
potential to become
our Father's offspring.
Thru our obedience to the
principle of repentance, we
enjoy the companionship of His
Spirit. By the covenant of baptism,
we take upon ourselves a new
name, which is His name, and
this cleansing prompts our
spiritual rebirth, so that
we may become
as He is.

When we content ourselves
with chokeberries, we deny ourselves
the unique and wonderful experience of
tasting Huckleberry Delight. Instead, we become
accustomed to the bitterness of its negative
counterpart. We become enthusiastically
ignorant, as we invent stories that
justify our support of the
chokeberry culture.

Our Father
provides a perfect
way for us to regain
and retain the warm
glow of our former
home, in a process
that He calls
repentance.

Our undeviating Exemplar is unlike those chameleon-like characters who peddle their birthright for a mess of pottage, negotiate their standards for a shot at stardom, and dilute the potency of their discipleship by adopting the values of vulgarity.

If we are not
careful, hypocrisy
can get under our skin;
it can worm its way right
into our hearts, minds, and souls
after our barrier protection has been
compromised. Unless we are quick
to repent, it can then distort our
celestial features into grotesque
caricatures that are nothing
more than the masks of
a hypocrite.

We cannot
go back to write
a new beginning, but we
can always start today and
begin a new ending. We can
re-boot the system, get rid of
bad code, and restore damaged
files. We can create enough RAM
and additional disk space to
write a bedtime story in
which we all live
happily ever
after.

Satan, and all who follow him, are most miserable. They are mired in their sins. They no longer enjoy the freedom to choose, rendering them powerless to alter either their circumstances or their unfortunate outcomes.

Satan uses
telestial trivia
that rely on the
treasures of the earth,
as counterfeit pleasures
for the blessing of happiness
that our Father in Heaven has
reserved for His repentant
children.

Without
our repentance,
we can get caught in
conceptually confusing
cul-de-sacs that prevent
us from comprehending the
purpose of life. We wander to
and fro, dazed and disoriented.
We risk becoming as flotsam
and jetsam, tossed about
without direction on
the sea of life.

God's perfect Plan has the depth, breadth, majesty, and capacity to encircle all His children within His tender embrace.

Those of weak character frequently think that they can side step the requirements of repentance, if only because they have never enjoyed the experiences of those who live on the strait and narrow path, thanks to the therapeutic and liberating influence of the Savior's Atonement.

Our
exercise
of repentance
triggers alarm
bells in heaven, to
get the immediate
and undivided
attention of
Father.

With our
repentance, we
throw ourselves upon
an altar of faith whose
foundation is buttressed
by a supernal display
of divine direction.

When we pass through the portal of baptism, our lives open up in an expansion of eternal opportunities as we obtain a remission of sins, gain membership in the Church, and are personally sanctified through the receipt of the Holy Ghost. We have the Spirit of God to be with us.

Repentance,
made possible
by the Atonement,
removes the stain of
sin from the tapestry
that is the tableau
of our lives.

Standing in opposition
to grace is a darkness that
is so great that it has the potential
to cover the earth, and gross darkness
the people. Without repentance and the
Atonement, we would be subject to the
evil source of that gloominess, to
rise no more.

Repentance
shepherds us thru
the growing pains and
mental, emotional, physical,
and spiritual instability that are
related to early childhood
development.

Righteousness
is always modest
in its appearance,
and its value is
enduring.

We are only
fully repentant when
we have charity, or the pure
love of Christ, and are strictly
obedient to the principle of
forgiveness, and that
door swings both
ways.

Repentance catalyzes a mystical and metaphysical transformation wherein we may be figuratively born of God.

The
beauty
of repentance
is that it meets
all of the demands
of perfect Justice thru
the infinite Mercy of
our Father in
Heaven.

If we allow ourselves
to become isolated from the
sensitivity to our surroundings
that is nurtured by repentance, we
may become inured to our condition
in the sense that we are past feeling.
If that is so, then the power of the
Atonement is of no effect in our
lives, and for us, the Savior of
the world suffered in the
Garden of Gethsemane
and died on the Cross
at Calvary, for
naught.

When we determine to repent, the Holy Spirit gives us fire for the deed.

The Devil's
enticements lead the
imprudent into conceptual
cul-de-sacs from which there
can be no exit save a stammering
shifting of blame, a frantic flight
from responsibility, rationalized
retreat, brazen back-pedaling,
and confused complacency
leading to a senseless
stupor of thought,
and unmitigated
defeat.

Repentance,
and the Atonement of
Christ, make life eternal,
love immortal, and death
only a horizon, which is
nothing, save the limit
of our sight.

Repentance
will always be waiting
in the wings, to be applied
as a balm to repair bruised
egos, bitter feelings, and
battered birthrights.

With repentance, and
thru the miracle of the infinite,
continuing, uninterrupted, unspoiled,
uncorrupted, enduring, unfathomable
and immeasurable grace of God, we
are swallowed up in joy, to the
exhausting of our strength.
(See Alma 27:17).

As the Sufi poet Rumi observed: "Our wounds become portals that allow light to enter us."

The
world does a
remarkable job
of rationalizing its
naughty behavior, re-
purposing its deviancy,
and redefining in new-
speak the acceptability of
its conduct, in efforts to
somehow circumvent the
Law of Compensation.

Repentance is one of those things in life that is almost too good to be true, but what makes it believable is the miracle of the Atonement.

The image and likeness of God to which the repentant aspire are reflections of His divine attributes and His noble character. They are marked by uncomplicated simplicity, a refreshing candor, unblemished honesty, and His undisputed holiness.

For the repentant, the Light of Christ casts a steady glow over the nursery that we now call home.

We can always
be reassured that in
each instance following
our repentance, we hear
the unassuming words of
the Savior: "Neither do
I condemn thee. Go,
and sin no more."
(John 8:11).

Converts often emerge from the refiner's fire after having had the spiritual equivalent of open-heart surgery, as the dross of their former lives is purged from their systems by the white hot fire of God that is manifest in the forgiveness of sin.

In one
of his epistles,
Paul affirmed that
it is only "the grace
of God that bringeth
salvation." (Titus 2:11).
Luke similarly taught:
"Through the grace of
the Lord Jesus Christ,
we shall be saved."
(Acts 15:11).

Prayer and repentance go hand-in-hand. We confess our faults and pray that we may be healed. Our fervent prayers can reach all the way to the courts of heaven.

Conscience is
a celestial spark
that God puts into
each of us; an element
of the Merciful Plan of
our Great Creator. Its
purpose is the saving
of our souls.

To rely upon our own impotent efforts to improve our lives, instead of upon the boundless grace of God that is epitomized by the principle of repentance, reduces The Plan to a crude caricature that is without meaning and substance.

About The Author

Phil Hudson and his wife Jan have 7 children and over 25 grandchildren. They enjoy spending time with their family at their cabin nestled in the Selkirk Mountains, on the shore of Priest Lake, the crown jewel of North Idaho. Phil had a successful dental practice in Spokane, Washington for 43 years, before retiring in 2015. He has an eclectic mix of hobbies, and enjoys the out of doors. He always finds time, however, to record his thoughts on his laptop, and understands Isaac Asimov's response when he was asked: If you knew that you had only 10 minutes left to live, what would you do?" He answered: "I'd type faster."

Phil received the inspiration to write this book while he and Jan were serving as missionaries for The Church of Jesus Christ of Latter-day Saints, in the Kingdom of Tonga. While there, they celebrated their 50th wedding anniversary.

In spite of our focus on accountability, agency, industry, and labor, and even as we are inspired to greater dedication, duty, and diligence, the simple truth is that nothing we do could ever qualify us to merit eternal life with our Father.

By The Author

Essays

    Volume One: Spray From The Ocean Of Thought
    Volume Two: Ripples On A Pond
    Volume Three: Serendipitous Meanderings
    Volume Four: Presents Of Mind
    Volume Five: Mental Floss
    Volume Six: Fitness Training For The Mind And Spirit

First Principles and Ordinances Series

    Faith – Our Hearts Are Changed Through Faith On His Name
    Repentance – A Broken Heart and a Contrite Spirit
    Baptism – One Hundred And One Reasons Why We Are Baptized
    The Holy Ghost – That We Might Have His Spirit To Be With Us
    The Sacrament – This Do In Remembrance Of Me

Book of Mormon Commentary

    Volume One: Born In The Wilderness
    Volume Two: Voices From The Dust
    Volume Three: Journey To Cumorah

Doctrine & Covenants Commentary

- Volume One – Sections 1 – 34
- Volume Two – Sections 35 – 57

Minute Musings: Spontaneous Combustions of Thought

- Volume One
- Volume Two
- Volume Three

Calendars:

- In His Own Words: Discovering William Tyndale
- As I Think About The Savior
- Scriptural Symbols

Children's Books

- Muddy, Muddy
- The Thirteen Articles of Faith
- Happy Birthday

Doctrinal Themes

    The House of the Lord

A Thought For Each Day Of The Year

    Faith
    Repentance
    Baptish
    The Holy Ghost
    The Sacrament
    The House Of The Lord
    The Atonement
    The Plan of Salvation

Professional Publications

    Diode Laser Soft Tissue Surgery Volume One
    Diode Laser Soft Tissue Surgery Volume Two
    Diode Laser Soft Tissue Surgery Volume Three

These, and other titles, are available from online retailers.

Without repentance, our spirits can become horribly disfigured by the evils that have been committed behind an illusory shield of invisibility.

Quid magis possum dicere?

www.ingramcontent.com/pod-product-compliance
Lightning Source LLC
Chambersburg PA
CBHW060508240426
43661CB00007B/950